Making
SOAP
for Fun *and* Profit

Linda Inlow

KOPACETIC INK • KALAMA, WA

Published and distributed in the United States by:
   Kopacetic inK,
   P O Box 323, Kalama, WA 98625
   (360) 673-1743 fax or
   email books@kalama.com

Edited by: Kathryn Doll
Photographs: Hidden Meadows Handcrafts

Library of Congress Catalog Card Number: 98-091683

ISBN 0-9619634-2-5

First Printing August 1998
Second Printing April 1999
Third Printing February 2000
Webcom

Printed in Canada

A special thanks to Kayln and David
who gave their mom enough time and space
to make the soap and write this book.

To Shelly Morgan, without whom
the first batch of soap would never have been made.

TABLE *of* CONTENTS

BASICS *of* MAKING SOAP

My GRANDMOTHER MADE SOAP FOR DOING THE LAUNDRY in her basement. I can still remember the pungent odor permeating the downstairs. I remember my hands feeling silky from playing with the flakes in her laundry soap box.

Later commercial soaps like Ivory and Life Boy became readily available in stores or from salesmen going door to door. The necessity to make one's own soap was pushed aside for modern convenience.

The advent of washing machines, dishwashers, and the "need" for different kinds of soap—hand soap, body bars, liquid soap, shower gels, and the like—created a vast new market for commercial soaps. It was not until the 1970's a few women began to 'get back to basics'; this included learning how to make soap.

Surprisingly the soap we use today is a fairly new addition to our culture and lifestyle. Before the 1800's soap was used primarily for laundering. It was not until this century that soap making became a strong commercial concern with recipes guarded and fragrances and colors added to the soap.

Today I make soap in the kitchen. It feels just as gentle and silky to the skin as my grandmother's. It definitely smells better than hers.

The recipes employed in this book are kind to the environment, use products from the herb or vegetable garden, utilize ingredients from the kitchen cupboard and incorporate fats or oils easily purchased from the grocery store. I began to make soap for gifts, then sold a few bars at the local open market and then to a few retail stores on the West Coast.

At the open market older people especially admire the soap and made comments such as, "You made the soap? I remember my grandmother making soap. Lye soap it was. It didn't smell or look this good! I've often thought about trying this at home."

Making soap can be a fun as well as practical adventure. Unlike the commercial soap makers who still guard their formulas, in this book I share recipes and techniques used in my kitchen. *Making Soap for Fun and Profit* presents a step by step process of making basic soaps and then explains how to create unique blends using various oils, additives, colorants, or essential oils.

ADDITIONAL READING:

The Natural Soap Book by Susan Miller Cavitch offers excellent detailed explanations of the chemistry involved in making soap as well as an extensive suppliers list.

Ann Bramson's *Soap, Making It, Enjoying It* details the history of soap making and offers a few recipes.

The Soap Book by Sandy Maine gives a little history and many delightful variations of one basic recipe.

There are only a few soap making books on the market. Each has a special focus. I would encourage the avid learner to read and compare.

If the soapmaker wants a quick foolproof way to make soap, simply purchase a ready made glycerin soap bar from a craft store. Melt glycerin in a pot, add scent (if necessary, many are pre-scented) and pour it into molds. Often molds are provided with this type of soap making kit. The more challenging way of making soap follows. Making soap by this method is more dangerous, than simply purchasing the glycerin soap making kit at a crafts store. The soapmaker handles a caustic material and caution *must* supersede action.

If the back-to-basics methods sounds more challenging, appealing, or you want to create something really unique the following materials are essential.

ESSENTIALS FOR SOAP MAKING:

2 WOODEN SPOONS or SPATULAS

Easy pour PLASTIC/GLASS CUP

RUBBER GLOVES

SAFETY GOGGLES

ACCURATE SCALE—up to 2 lb.

APRON or "soap outfit"

NEWSPAPER

Blankets

ENAMEL or STAINLESS STEEL POT (at least 4 qt)

　　not aluminum, cast iron or tin

VINEGAR

2 CUP plastic or glass MEASURING CUP

2 THERMOMETERS (80°-140°F)

2 QUART CANNING GLASS JAR

Molds

Boxes

STAINLESS STEEL WIRE WHISK

Keep in mind the location for making soap. Work in a well lit area with a sink, plenty of counter space and ventilation.

Lay newspapers on the floor and countertops to protect surface from the lye/soap solution. The lye can burn the floor; if some spills, wipe up immediately.

Once the essentials and ingredients are in order it should take between one and half and two hours to make a batch of soap.

INGREDIENTS TO HAVE ON HAND:

VARIOUS OILS and/or FATS

100% LYE e.g. Red Devil

WATER—distilled, spring, or tap

ESSENTIAL OILS or PERFUMES

HERBS (optional)
SPICES FOR COLOR (optional)
FIRST AID KIT: Vinegar and warm water
Exfoliants (optional)

LYE IS TOXIC AND A VERY CAUSTIC CHEMICAL!

Lye is simply sodium hydroxide. It can be found in granular or flake form. Lye reacts very quickly when in contact with the skin. It can leave a serious chemical burn, if unattended. Keep the "first aid kit" near the soap making process. To counteract the high alkalinity use an acid fluid like vinegar, orange juice or carbonated soda pop on the burn. Rinse the area with warm water. Repeat if the area still feels like it's burning.

The equipment is gathered, the ingredients chosen,, the soap-maker acts with caution and begins to make soap!

Basic Instructions *for* Making Soap

LYE: Measure lye (amount depends on recipe) into a glass jar, add cold or tepid water slowly and mix well. Be sure the container is large enough in case an adverse chemical reaction occurs. I usually use a two quart Kerr canning jar—twice the size of my final liquid. This is especially important when using an herbal infusion (tea). It can "boil up" and create an overflow, much like mixing soda and ice cream. The overflow is *caustic, toxic* as well as messy.

Keep head and eyes averted when pouring. The fumes are highly toxic and may cause dizziness, headache or nausea.

Early Preparation
Fats and/or lye solution can be made a day ahead!

- To increase temperature place the lye or pot of fat in a sink with two inches of hot water. Stir prior to taking the temperature as heat pockets can localize.

- To decrease temperature put lye or fats in the sink or larger container of cold water. Stir to avoid cold spots, prior to measuring the temperature.

Set aside (preferably in a well-ventilated area—outside is okay). *Keep children and pets away from the mixture.* **Always wear rubber gloves and goggles when handling the lye and/or solution.**

FATS: Weigh and measure the fats; melt *solid* fats in an enamel or stainless steel pot over low heat. As soon as the fats melt remove from heat. Add any additional *liquid* fats, i.e. olive oil, soybean, walnut.

MOLDS: Prepare molds and surfaces while fats are melting if not done previously. Grease molds with shortening, mineral oil or pan spray. PVC pipe with one end closed, juice containers, milk cartons, shoe boxes, rubber storage containers, and candy molds, work well as containers for the saponifying mixture. DO NOT use metal containers, unless covered with plastic lining. Fancy or basic soap molds may usually be purchased at a crafts supply store.

MIXING: Monitor fats and lye solution with thermometers. Stir the mixture prior to taking the measurement. Ideal temperatures for mixing are 95°F to 98°F. Many soapmakers mix when the fats are a few degrees higher than the lye/water solution.

Wearing rubber gloves pour lye solution in a thin steady stream into the melted fats. Stir[1] constantly in a circular motion. Note the change in color and consistency. A chemical reaction has begun called *saponification*. This chemical reaction actually makes the soap, turning the lye/fat solution into the natural by-products of glycerin and soap. In manufactured soaps, most of the glycerin is removed and sold to various industries. Handmade soap retains the natural glycerin, giving it special properties and a different texture from store-bought soaps.

SAPONIFICATION: Continue to stir until a "trace" forms. "Trace" occurs when the saponification leaves a pattern or impression when a drop of the soap mixture stays on top or when the spoon traces a design in the mixture, or when the mixture feels like a thickened pudding or gravy. This can take up to 1½ hours. Count on 10 to 20 minutes for most of the following recipes.

ADDITIVES: (optional): After a trace has formed add herbs, exfoliating agents, spices or essential oils. Stir quickly, blend well, then pour into molds. ***Remember to wear rubber gloves throughout this process.***

Hint: Do not let the soap cool too quickly. This could cause separation of the oils in the soap.

---

[1] *Stir with a wooden spoon or spatula. To speed the process an electric mixer or hand mixer with stainless steel blade may be used. Use a deep pot to avoid excessive splashing.*

STORAGE: Store molds in a box or covered container. Surround with blankets, newspapers, towels or styrofoam. Do not disturb for at least 18-24 hours. The coverings can be removed after 18 hours **but** do not cut or shape for at least another six hours.

CUT: Remove from molds, cut into bars or shapes. Recipes calling for 60-64 ounces of fat will make approximately 40 two ounce bars of soap. Stack the soap in a loose pyramid style in a box. This lets the air circulate. Leave in the box for another two to three weeks.

A test for readiness: if your tongue doesn't tingle to the touch of the soap it is ready for use!!

After two weeks there may be a white residue on the soap. This is soda ash. It may dry the skin, but doesn't mean the soap is spoiled. Brush it or cut it off. This residue has been used in the laundry with good results, especially on white clothing.

Although it may sound tedious, it generally takes only one and a half to two hours to make a batch of soap. The following five basic recipes make generally hard, mild, white body bars. From these recipes the adventuresome soapmaker can make colorful soaps, fragrant soaps, exfoliating soaps or, in other words, enjoy *making soap for fun or profit!*

Five Basic Soap Recipes

All the soap recipes in this
book are Lye Heavy if using
a measuring cup to measure
the Lye; they are Lye Heavy
also using a Digital Scale.

Go online and check these
Recipes using the "MMS Soap Calculator".
This calculator bases its measurements
on using a Digital Scale and
most soap recipes on-line are based
on Digital Scale — not measuring cup.
Always check a recipe on MMS
(Majestic Mountain Sage) Soap
Calculator.

CASTILE SOAP

This is one of the oldest recipes for soap. It is named for the Castilla region in Spain, an area rich in the production of olive oil. This region kept a hold on the soap market for several decades until other European regions, rich in olive oil, entered the competition.

The soap is hard and white. This soap must be cut as soon as it hardens. It may become brittle with age and will not cut as well later. This soap is not known for its' lather. The recipe has traced very quickly in the past (five minutes!).

11.5 ounces lye
32 ounces water (distilled, rain or tap)
60 ounces tallow
26 ounces olive oil

Tallow Plus Soap

Blending the tallow with olive and coconut oil this soap still remains brittle to cut but becomes rich, creamy, and bubbly in the bath! The coconut oil creates the bubble effect in all soaps. Most of the commercial soaps are made with coconut oil and tallow *without* olive oil. The olive oil enriches the lather and is soothing to the skin.

24 ounces coconut oil
24 ounces olive oil
38 ounces tallow
12 ounces lye
32 ounces water

VEGETARIAN SOAP

This soap is very inexpensive to make since no costly oils are involved in the process. It takes about twenty minutes or less to trace.

62 ounces vegetable shortening
32 ounces distilled water
11.5 ounces lye

VEGETABLE SOAP
BASE I

This soap combines the lathering quality of coconut, with equal amount of olive oil and uses vegetable shortening in the base. Vegetable base soap is very mild. It takes exfoliating agents, colorants, essential oils, and herbs very easily. This allows the soapmaker a never ending variety. This soap takes on average about fifteen minutes to trace. The temperature of the kitchen and the weather may affect tracing times.

24 ounces coconut oil
24 ounces olive oil
38 ounces vegetable shortening
12 ounces lye
32 ounces water

VEGETABLE SOAP II

This one is more creamy than the first vegetable soap, but also more expensive to make.

44 ounces olive oil
17 ounces coconut oil
24 ounces vegetable shortening
11 ounces lye
32 ounces water

Although not highly recommended, these recipes can be halved or quartered. Greater success has come from doubling the recipe.

Notes

The Fatty Oils

LYE, WATER, AND OIL are the *only* ingredients required to make soap. The lye changes only in volume, never content. The water base may be rainwater, distilled water, tap water, or an infused tea. A base fat can be from animal or vegetable. To this base other oils may be added, blended, or exchanged. Different oils may alter the texture and/or add fragrance to the soap.

How the soapmaker mixes and matches these various ingredients brings wonder, aroma, and genuine satisfaction in creating a usable and environmentally friendly product. Feel free to experiment with the various kinds of oil blends. Be sure the combined volume of oils does not exceed the total amount indicated in the original recipe.

The following table lists various oils, the consistency of the soap, and the natural color of the final product.

Tallow	Very very hard	Yellowish	Very mild soap
Coconut Oil	By itself very hard brittle soap	White to yellow	Can be drying
Olive Oil	Hard	Yellow to light green	Very mild soap
Avocado Oil	Softer soap than olive	White	Very mild soap
Palm Oil	Very hard, brittle	White to yellow	Very mild soap
Peanut Oil	Softer than olive	Light yellow	Very mild soap
Walnut Oil	Softer than olive	Light yellow	Mild soap
Soybean Oil	Hard	Light yellow to green	Mild
Shortening	Hard	White	Very mild soap

Homemade soaps are biodegradable, friendly to the environment, and loaded with natural glycerin—a by product often sold to cosmetic or drug companies by commercial soap makers!

The oils may be mixed and matched to create a special blend, color, or fragrance. It is not advised to use purely liquid oils when making the soap. A solid fat like tallow, lard, or various shortenings should be considered in creating the recipe.

Vegetable shortening, olive oil and coconut oil are readily available to make soap. Tallow is created from animal fat. Depending on location the animal fat may be purchased from a grocery store, butcher or rendering plant.

Purchase at least twice the weight of fat called for in the recipe. More tallow than necessary can be made and refrigerated or frozen for future use.

Some of the oils can be found at the local grocery store. Others are available in large quantities at grocery outlets.

Sometimes the local grocer will special order a particular oil.

More often specialty oils will be sold by essential oil wholesale or retail shops.

Cut the fat into small pieces. Heat over a low flame for several hours. Stir intermittently to avoid burning the fat. Most of the fat will liquefy, however some solid particles will remain. Using a colander or cheesecloth strain the fat and refrigerate or begin to clarify.

Rendering is the process of melting and purifying solid fats.

Clarifying means separating the true fat from the water and cracklings formed while under refrigeration

TO CLARIFY place the fat, an equal amount of water and 2 tablespoons of salt in a pan. Bring this mixture to a boil. Remove from the stove. Cool slightly, and add cold water—about 1 quart per gallon of hot liquid. Refrigerate until fat is solid—usually 6-8 hours or overnight. The mixture will separate into three layers; pure fat at the top, fat with impurities next, and water at the bottom. When the fat has formed on the top simply poke a small hole through the layers and drain out the water. Invert the remaining fat and cracklings on a flat surface. Scrape off the impure layer (cracklings). If the fat is rancid or foul smelling it may still be used just add one part vinegar to 5 parts of water in the clarifying process. The smell will dissipate.

Some of the oils have a distinctive odor that can be detected once the soap is made or when used. Tallow has a fatty odor; peanut oil smells like peanuts. You can use the odor to your advantage or mask it with essential oils.

SUPERFATTING Adding warmed cocoa butter or butter to the soap mixture prior to pouring it into molds is called *superfatting*. Superfatted soap is creamier and milder than regular hand-made soaps. The warmed oil does not saponify with the other oils so it can be used as an emollient in the soap.

Following are a few sample recipes mixing these fatty oils into specialty soaps.

Do not be afraid to mix and match the fatty oils for other unique creations.

AVOCADO SOAP

7 oz avocado oil
12 oz coconut oil
26 oz olive oil
36 oz vegetable shortening
32 oz water
12 oz lye

To color this very pleasant mild soap consider adding 1 to 2 ounces of fresh fennel crushed. It becomes a very light green with dark green flecks. The addition of fennel will add a mild exfoliating agent, but no scent.

To superfat add an additional 1 to 2 oz of avocado oil just prior to pouring into molds.

This could be a very gentle facial soap.

Variation: Instead of using avocado oil replace it with 7 ounces of either coconut, olive or shortening and add a real avocado just prior to pouring into the molds. Mash a medium avocado into a liquid using a blender or food processor, then add enough water to equal 9 ounces. Add 2 tsp. of powdered benzoin.

PEANUT OIL BASE SOAP

6 oz peanut oil
6 oz coconut
13 oz olive oil
18 oz shortening
16 oz water
6 oz. lye

For fun consider adding up to 3 tablespoons of cocoa. The soap comes out a deep chocolate fudge color. Chocoholics and children love this soap.

Bathing is a kid's delight. The suds are a rich brown—but the child comes out clean! The adult bather can savor the smells of cocoa and peanuts and not gain an ounce!

Although difficult to locate, a chocolate scent may be added to further the festivities in using this soap.

WALNUT OIL

6 oz walnut oil
6 oz coconut oil
13 oz olive oil
18 oz vegetable shortening
16 oz water
6 oz lye

Walnut oil has a very mild nutty fragrance. Unless natural colorants or essential oils are added to the soap it is a rather drab off-white, soft to cut, but hardens quickly during the curing stage.

PALM SOAP

24 ounces olive oil
24 ounces palm oil
38 ounces vegetable shortening
12 oz lye
32 oz water

A well-known commercial soap "Palmolive" came from blending these two oils.

Soybean Soap

24 ounces olive oil
12 ounces soybean oil
12 ounces coconut oil
38 ounces vegetable shortening
12 ounces lye
32 ounces water

One well-known micro-soap company uses the soybean/coconut/olive oil as their base recipe. This ivory colored soap easily takes fragrance and natural colorants.

LAVENDER-ALMOND SOAP

24 ounces olive oil
24 ounces coconut oil
38 ounces vegetable shortening
12 ounces lye
32 ounces water

Fragrance
2 ounces lavender essential oil
1 teaspoon bitter almond essential oil
¼ cup warm melted cocoa butter (superfatting)

This soap recipe uses the superfatting technique. The essential oils and warmed fatty oil are added just prior to pouring the soap into molds.

Lavender/Almond is hard and white. It has a delightfully mild almond/lavender fragrance. Bitter almond is a very strong scent and can overpower the gentle scent of the lavender if increased.

Notes

Additives

MOST ADDITIVES are usually put in the soap for exfoliating or emollient purposes. Most of the additives come from the kitchen cupboard or art supply store. Some of the most common are: bran, oatmeal (flakes or crushed), cornmeal, honey, milk, pumice, berries, seeds, and some herbs. These ingredients are added just prior to pouring the soap into molds.

Most of these recipes make about 38 - 40 two ounce bars of soap. It is possible to make one basic batch of soap, divide it into equal parts and put different additives in each for a wider variety. The following additives, except honey, will give the soap a slightly rough texture. Any of the additives may alter the color of the soap slightly.

RECOMMENDED AMOUNTS BASED ON A FULL RECIPE:

ADDITIVE	MEASUREMENT
Grains: oatmeal, cornmeal, bran	Maximum 4 ounces
Honey	Maximum 3 tablespoons
Milk—whole, non-fat, buttermilk	Maximum 3 tablespoons
Herbs	Maximum 2 ounces
Berries—crushed	Maximum 6 tablespoons
Cosmetic grade clay	Maximum 8 ounces
Pumice	Maximum 8 ounces

Kayln's Facial Soap

This is a delightfully mild exfoliating soap and a favorite for those with facial skin problems. It is unscented and inexpensive to make. It has even been used on kids with chicken pox.

4 cups solid vegetable shortening
20 level teaspoons lye
2 cups water

Additives
2 ounces of oatmeal (whole or crushed)
2 teaspoons of cinnamon powder for color (optional)

Honey Oatmeal

This too is a wonderful facial soap. Although primarily used as a facial soap, it is a very gentle body bar. It smells like oatmeal cookies! *Note: If too much honey is added, the soap will remain soft and mushy for weeks.*

4 cups vegetable shortening
2 cups water (distilled, tap or rain)
20 level teaspoons of lye

Additives
2 ounces oatmeal (crushed or whole)
2 tablespoons honey

KITCHENMAID

In this recipe an essential oil and grain are added. The slight citrus smell and mild exfoliating action cuts quickly through dirt and grime. It can be a hand or body bar.

4 cups vegetable shortening
2 cups water (distilled, tap or rain)
20 level teaspoons of lye

Fragrance
1 teaspoon orange or lemon (optional)

Additives
2 ounces cornmeal (powdered or whole)

ROSEMARY/DILL

A favorite body and facial bar. The fresh dill and rosemary serve two purposes: exfoliating agents and natural colorant. Rosemary is excellent for oily skin.

The herbs are fragrant and so is this soap. Many cooks leave the bars sitting in the kitchen for a delightful fresh scent.

38 ounces vegetable shortening
24 ounces coconut oil
24 ounces olive oil
32 ounces rainwater (distilled or tap)
11.5 ounces lye

Fragrance
3 ounces rosemary essential oil
1 ounce dill essential oil

Additives
3 ounces of a rosemary and dill weed blend

Note: Dried herbs work best in this recipe. The blend can be 50/50 or any combination based on personal preference or availability of the herb. Be sure to add no more than a combined total of 3 ounces.

BERRY BERRY

Berry soap is completely natural. Almost any berry can be used. The scent of the berry is not strong, but the seeds are wonderful as exfoliating agents. The berries may be freshly picked or frozen (but thawed before use). The soapmaker may be surprised at the final color of the soap.

4 cups shortening
1/4 cup olive oil
2 cups water
20 tsp. lye (level teaspoons)

Additives
6 tablespoons crushed blueberries or blackberries
1 to 2 ounces oatmeal
(turns amber with seed flecks)

or 4 tablespoons crushed raspberries
(becomes white with red flecks)
1 cup crushed oatmeal

Colorants

NATURAL COLORANTS keep the soap chemically free and often surprise the soapmaker at the outcome!

Consider using fruits, vegetables, bark, leaves, roots, flowers, and herbs as sources of color for the soap. When considering vegetables use fresh rather than canned. Salt and other additives can interfere with the how the soap is colored.

These natural ingredients cannot be added as solids to the soap, rather a tea (infusion) needs to be made and introduced in one of two ways.

The first is to use the tea in place of some of the water when preparing the lye solution. In a large container dissolve the lye in less water than required. Add enough of the colored tea to make up the difference. When temperatures are appropriate add to the fat solution.

The second method is to add a concentration of the colored tea just prior to pouring the soap into molds. This additional water will add some time to the drying period of the soap. Try to add no more than an ounce..

Marbling: Instead of mixing the colored soap back to the original, pour the uncolored soap into molds and dribble, pour or dabble the colored soap over the top. Leave as is or cut in with a knife. This gives a unique and beautiful pattern to the soap.

Be aware the chemical reaction with the lye may create a color the soapmaker didn't expect. The color will generally be lighter than the initial blending.

The soapmaker can use dry ingredients to color the soap. Spices and herbs from the kitchen cupboard are a nice alternative. Instead of pouring the powder directly into the soap mixture, pre-mix it with a small amount in another container. Blend it well with a wire whisk. When fully blended pour back into the soap or use the colored soap to marble the main batch.

Artificial dyes may be used to color soaps. Several soapmakers have found the candle dyes easily accessible and effective. These artificial colorants tend to be more predictable than natural counterparts. Food coloring can be used, but must be blended *very well* before pouring into molds.

NATURAL COLORS

Add no more than an ounce of powdered colorant to the soap. The amount added does effect the outcome: the more colorant used the darker the color. When using a liquid form of natural colorant i.e. infused tea add no more than 9 ounces. Some, like lettuce or carrot, need at least 6 ounces to be effective.

Cinnamon	Orange to Brown
Turmeric	Yellow
Paprika	Red to Brown
Cocoa	Brown to Chocolate
Chlorophyll	Green
Sage	Green to a musty Gray Green
Powdered Beet	Pink to Rose
Hibiscus	Rose to Purple
Powdered Orange Peel	Yellow
Fennel	Green
Dill	Light to Dark Green
Rosemary	Green
Mint	Light Green
Ginger	Light Caramel
Blackberry/Blueberry	Light Mustard
Lettuce	Very light green
Carrot	Light orange
Rosehips	Light to deep magenta

LEMON THAI

Infuse lemon Thai tea with two cups of water. Strain. Pour the tea infusion slowly into the glass jar containing the lye. There will be a strong bubbling reaction.

The soap has a light ivory/yellow color.

2 cups shortening
2 cups lemon Thai tea
20 teaspoons lye

Additives
2 ounces oatmeal
1 teaspoon yellow food coloring

STRAWBERRY

2 cups shortening
2 cups distilled water
20 teaspoons lye

Colorant
1 teaspoon red food coloring

Fragrance
½ fluid ounce strawberry essence *(not an extract)*

This is a bright pink soap with just a hint of strawberry essence. Kids, especially, seem to enjoy this soap.

Cool Mint

A cooling sensation to sensitive skin this light green soap adds a fresh scent to the bath, kitchen or car!

19.5 ounces vegetable shortening
12 ounces coconut oil
12 ounces olive oil
2 cups rainwater
20 level teaspoons lye

Fragrance
1 fluid ounce each peppermint and spearmint

Colorant
½ cup dried peppermint or 1 tsp. chlorophyll

Alternative: Use 2 ounces of only one mint essential oil

HOLSTEIN SOAP

Special instructions: Pour half the soap mixture into the molds after adding the fragrance. Quickly mix the cocoa into the remaining soap. Drizzle over the molds. Cut in with wooden spoon or knife for marbling effect.

3 cups shortening
1 cup coconut oil
2 cups freezing cold rainwater
20 teaspoons lye

Fragrance
1 fluid ounce jasmine essential oil

Colorant
3 tablespoons cocoa

Note: For round bars place a heavy piece of cardboard down the middle of the tube. Pour "white" soap on one side; pour the "black" on the other. As the cardboard is slowly lifted from the tube, twist for a swirled effect or lift slowly for a half and half. This technique works best with two people.

LUMBERJACK

Lumberjack is a very dark musty green with a woodsy fragrance.
The Northwest forests inspired its creation.

19 ounces vegetable shortening
12 ounces coconut oil
12 ounces olive oil
6 ounces lye
16 ounces water (tap, rain or distilled)

Fragrance
1 oz sage essential oil
3 teaspoons white pine
1 teaspoon pettigrain

Colorant
.6 ounces ground sage

ALL NATURAL SOAP

19 ounces vegetable shortening
12 ounces coconut oil
12 ounces olive oil
6 ounces lye
16 ounces water (tap, rain or distilled)

Colorant
1 cup rosehips infused

Special instructions: Infuse 1 cup of rosehips in boiling water. Let stand for at least three hours. Strain. Pour the thick liquid into the soap mixture just prior to pouring into molds. If it is not stirred (whisks work well) completely the soap will have a pink marbled effect.

Essential Oils

ESSENTIAL OILS add character, fragrance, and benefits to home-made soap. They can be purchased through health stores or supply houses. It is possible to make essential oils. The volume required for extraction may seem a bit prohibitive for the at-home consumer, for example it takes 12,000 pounds of jasmine flowers to produce 2 pounds of oil!

It requires a large amount of flowers to produce even an ounce of oil—but it can be done! One of the easiest way to extract is to soak the herb or flowers in oil. Strangely enough, oil attracts oil.

Oil may also be extracted by using undenatured ethyl alcohol. If this type of alcohol is difficult to locate, vodka may be substituted. The extraction process is the same as for oil (see sidebar p.44). The fragrant alcohol may be used as is or diluted with some water. The end product makes a very nice natural perfume.

OIL BASED EXTRACTION

Place blossoms in a sealed bottle. Use a nonmetal or ceramic container. Pour pure oil or safflower oil to cover the blossoms.

Set aside for 24 hours.

Strain by gently pressing the blossoms.

Add more blossoms to the fragrant oil.

Repeat at least six times.

The end result may be used in soaps, baths, lotions, potpourris.

Be sure to store in a tightly covered container.

To remove the oil from the alcohol, freeze it. The oil solidifies and can be easily separated from the alcohol.

The most useful herbal oils are essential oils. They are usually extracted by steam distillation. This process, too, can be done at home, but it is far easier to purchase essential oils from the store or wholesaler (see sidebar).

What constitutes a perfect blend is a matter of personal preference. The combinations in the following recipes came about through happenstance and availability of the oils with some delightful results. When purchasing essential oils avoid those labeled "perfume" or "potpourri" oils. Essential oils by their very nature are very concentrated. Not all essential oils are good for skin care.

Some suggestions in using essential oils for skincare are:

- Normal Skin: geranium, lavender, lemon, ylang-ylang, cedarwood
- Dry Skin: cedarwood, orange, sandalwood, ylang-ylang, peppermint
- Oily Skin: cedarwood, lavender, orange, patchouli, sandalwood, lemon
- Acne Prone: cedarwood, geranium, lavender, patchouli, peppermint, tea tree
- Excema: cedarwood, eucalyptus, lavender, patchouli, ylang-ylang

Many of these oils are fairly easy to find. The more common essential oils like cedarwood, jasmine, lavender, eucalyptus, orange, and ylang-ylang may be purchased at health food centers and craft stores. If used in larger amounts the soapmaker should seek a local oil wholesaler or low end retail store in the area. These stores carry hundreds of essential oils, perfume oils, and fatty oils.

Again, what kind and what combination of oils to use in the soap making process is entirely open to individual preference, experimentation, and pocketbook. Some essential oils are *very* expensive. Like the coffee market, price fluctuates based on availability and season.

There follows a suggested list of blends to use with the soapmakers favorite basic recipe. Experiment with personal favorites. Try not to exceed four fluid ounces in recipes which make 38 - 40 bars! The excess oil could be floating on the top.

The following recipes offer the soapmaker many delightful alternatives and fragrant blends. Don't be afraid to experiment with favorite fragrances of your own.

AROMA VERA CO. PO Box 3609 Culver city, CA 90231 (213) 675-8219

ESSENTIAL OIL CO. PO Box 206 Lake Oswego, OR 97038 1-800-729-5912 email order @essentialoil.com

FRONTIER HERB COOPERATIVE Box 299 Norway, Iowa 52318 1-800-669-3275

LAVENDER LANE 7337 #1 Roseville Rd Sacramento, CA 95842 1-888-593-4400 low-end retail

LIBERTY NATURAL PRODUCTS 8120 SE Stark Portland, OR 97215 1-800-289-8427 www.libertynatural.com

note: use the internet yellow pages to find essential oil companies in a specific area.

OLD SHAVING SOAP

The lather is reminiscent of the old shaving soap, mug and brush. This naturally caramel colored soap is a great body bar as well. This soap, too, has been used as a room and car freshener. The cinnamon scent is invigorating!

38 ounces vegetable shortening
24 ounces coconut oil
24 ounces olive oil
32 ounces rainwater
11.5 ounces lye

Fragrance
4 fluid ounces cinnamon leaf essential oil

FARMER JOHN SOAP

Farmer John has a mild pleasing scent. Works great on a gardener's grimy hands.

38 ounces vegetable shortening
24 ounces coconut oil
24 ounces olive oil (added later)
32 ounces rainwater (tap or distilled)
11.5 ounces lye

Fragrance
4 fluid ounce lemon essential oil
1 fluid ounce cedarwood oil

SERENITY SOAP

According to aromatherapists lavender invokes serenity. It has a calming and relaxing influence. This is one of the most popular fragrances used in soapmaking. Its mild aroma carries subtle properties and combines well with other herbs and spices.

3 cups shortening
1 cup coconut oil
2 cups rainwater
20 teaspoons lye

Fragrance
1 fluid ounce lavender essential oil
½ fluid ounce rosemary essential oil

Makes @ 20 2 ounce bars

HERBALED SPICE

Herbaled spice is a very strong scented naturally amber colored soap. The cassia essential oil gives a strong cinnamon presence in the soap.

19 ounces vegetable shortening
24 ounces coconut oil
24 olive oil
11 ounces lye
32 ounces water (distilled, rain or tap)

Fragrance
6 teaspoons thyme essential oil
8 teaspoons clove essential oil
8 teaspoons lavender essential oil
8 teaspoons pettigrain essential oil
24 teaspoons cassia essential oil

Additive
1 ounce cornmeal

JASMINE

The scent of jasmine invigorates and revitalizes the senses. A little bit goes a long way.

3 cups shortening
1 cup coconut oil
2 cups rainwater
20 teaspoons lye

Fragrance
1 fluid ounce jasmine essential oil

Additive
1 oz oatmeal

Makes @ 20 2 ounce bars.

More Special Blends

Each batch should yield @ 40 2 ounce bar recipes or 5 pounds of soap

Blend	Essential Oils	Amount
Mystical Forest	Sandalwood	2 ounces
	Patchouli	1 ounce
	Sassafras	½ ounce
	Pettigrain	1 teaspoon
California Citrus	Lemon	1 ounce
	Orange	½ ounce
	Bergamont	½ ounce
	Lemongrass	½ ounce
	Clove	½ teaspoon
Surprise!	Cedarwood	2 ounces
	Verbena	1 ounce
	Bitter Almond	½ ounce
Evergreen	Mountain Pine	1 ounce
	Cedar	2 ounces
	Sage	½ ounce
Bouquet	Lavender	2 ounces
	Rose	1 ounce
Old World	Juniper Berry	1 ounce
	Thyme	1 ounce
	Lavender	1 ounce
	Rosemary	½ ounce
	Vanilla	1 teaspoon
	Bitter Almond	½ teaspoon
Hot Stuff	Cassia	2 ounces
	Clove	1 ounces
	Almond	½ teaspoon
Highlander	Lavender	2 ounces
	Rosemary	1 ounce
	Juniper Berry	½ ounce

Harvest Time	Apple Blossom	2 ounces
	Lavender	1 ounce
	Pettigrain	½ ounce
	Cedarwood	½ ounce
David's Solace	Lavender	1 ounce
	Patchouli	1 ounce
	Oakmoss	1 ounce
Hidden Pleasure	Lavender	2 ounces
	Vanilla	1½ ounces
	Patchouli	1 ounce
Aloha Spice	Lemon Verbena	1½ ounces
	Sassafras	1 ounce
	Clove	½ ounce
Dr. Mom	Eucalyptus	3 ounces
	Mint	1 ounce

Cut *and* Wrap

AFTER TWENTY-FOUR HOURS THE SOAP may be removed from its' mold. If a special mold was used the soap already has a definite shape and size. If the mold was a large rectangular box, tube, carton or can, the soap needs to be cut and/or shaped.

The easiest cut is a straight line using a piece of wire, knife, or serrated utensil. Depending on the mold the bar will either be cut in a square, rectangle, or circle. To give them a fancier edge, each of these shapes can be beveled (small sections cut at a 45° away from the edges) on one side or all. Each cut will add character. Of course the soap can be left plain.

If using a milk carton as a mold consider cutting the soap into squares. You may then want to cut the squares into triangles. An attractive and unusual gift is tying two different triangle soaps together in the shape of a square!

Once the soap is cut, the soapmaker may want to wrap it, shape it or decorate the soap to make it more attractive. If the soap is soft enough, mold the soap into balls with your hands. Consider one of the following methods:

· before pouring soap into molds place fresh herbs in bottom; when inverted the herbs make an attractive top!

· use a plastic or glass soap dish as mold; leave soap in the dish!

MOLDS CAN BE PURCHASED FROM CRAFT STORES OR

Pourette
6910 Roosevelt Way NE
Seattle, WA 98115
(206) 525-4488

- juice cans

- quart milk cartons

- half-gallon cartons

- shoe boxes

- various size plastic storage containers

- PVC pipe—different dimensions

- solid peach crates lined with kitchen garbage bags

- place shapes, doilies, leaves, anything decorative in bottom of the mold; their pattern will imprint on the soap

- wrap in fabric

- carve the soap into special shapes

- completely wrap in colored or plain plastic wrap

- leave ends open when wrapping for look and scent

- melt glycerin soap and dribble over soap or coat top layer; sprinkle fresh herbs, flowers or leaves; let harden and cut away excess

- wrap in colored tissue paper

- cut again with a special serrated knife

- tie with ribbon or raffia

- make a soap basket assortment

- place in an attractive container or dish

How Soap Came To Be

CLEANLINESS MAY BE NEXT TO GODLINESS, but it has not always been achieved with the use of soap. Cosmetics, essences and oils were used to deodorize and "cleanse" the body long before soap was discovered.

Cleopatra used essential oils to mask odors and fine white sand to abrasively clean her skin. The infamous Roman baths also used essences and oils for bathing, but alas little soap.

Historically it seems the Arabs and then the Turks were the first to use soap as we know it. As nations conquered or were conquered the knowledge of soap and its use spread. Soap and water as cleansing methods did not become commonplace until the 13th Century. A plentiful supply of olive oil and barilla (a fleshy plant whose ashes were used to make lye) were important in making cities great centers of soapmaking. Marseilles was the first great center. Genoa, Venice and Bari in Italy soon came to rival it as did Castilla in Spain.

Poor olive harvests in the early 1700's affected the manufacturing of soap. Soapmakers experimented and found other oils besides olive to use in their soaps. As means of transportation flourished the importation of other oils became practical. Soap was soon being made with a blend of oils.

Soapmaking as an industry began soon after Nicholas LeBlanc discovered a process for manufacturing soda ash from brine (a type of salt). Before this time it was leached from wood ashes, a very slow and inefficient method of making the lye.

Even so, most of the soap made during this period was for laundry and not personal use. Not until the 18th Century when bathing was practiced as a medical and restorative treatment did the populace even consider using it for cleansing the body.

As the 18th Century progressed water took on magical properties and with it the use of soap. As more physicians prescribed baths for health the elite and others began bathing for pleasure.

With the technological advances of plumbing, including running water and draining bathtubs, the soap industry experienced greater and greater prosperity.

Making soap in the "early days" of the United States of America was a once a year process. Housewives saved the fat and scraps of meat with fat for an entire year. They leached their lye from ashes. Sometime during the year (usually summer) the heavy pots would be brought out and the fat scraps transformed into tallow. Over an open fire they would guess the temperatures and combine the fats with the lye and commence making their yearly soap supply.

In the cities and growing rural neighborhoods soap sellers would come and sell soap door to door. Some of the first soap sellers in the United States traded and bargained their wares. They would take the fat supply from housewives and return with soap. William Procter and James Gamble were soap sellers in Cincinnati, Ohio. Much later soap like theirs could be purchased in blocks or chipped off a large block and sold by weight at the general store.

After a few years their distribution and manufacturing of soap grew. Soon they were selling their products up and down the Ohio river. In 1879 they began distributing and advertising their famed Ivory soap.

They were not the only soap sellers to make it big. Out west the B.J. Johnson Company began making soap from palm and olive oil. Their first soap combined both of these names—Palm-olive. The soap was so popular they changed their company name to Palmolive. The original soap is not the same as the soap and detergent used today.

In the latter 19th century the Lever brothers of England joined the United States soap market with the manufacturing of and distributing the now infamous Lifeboy soap.

In 1806 William Colgate started a soapmaking business in New York. Colgate & Company became one of the first major soap making concerns in the United States. In the 1830's the company began selling individual bars in uniform weights. It wasn't until 1872 Colgate introduced Cashmere Bouquet, a perfumed soap!

With the growth of the soap business came mergers and take-overs. In 1928 Palmolive merged with Peet and soon after Colgate company. It wasn't until 1953 the Palmolive-Peet-Colgate company became simply Colgate-Palmolive.

Some of the classic advertisements for these soaps that became household words are replicated in Ann Bramson's book, *Soap*.

The fledging soap companies of the early 1900's concentrated on laundry soap. The soap industry today is incredibly varied. There are different soaps for different needs—dishwasher, car, boat, liquid, powder, shower, or bath to name a few.

With the growth of the soap industry, especially during World War II, the environment suffered. Synthetic cleaning agents developed during this time caused massive pollution of many of the world's waterways.

The earlier, more natural soaps consisted of molecules broken down by natural bacteria. These synthetic products were not broken down completely and made maintaining clean waterways next to impossible. Pollution escalated when phosphates were introduced to commercial soaps. Today most of the major soap companies are attempting to manufacture soaps which are, once again, gentle to the environment.

Homemade soap has become a welcome addition to many craft, florist, and bath stores. Soaps made by hand are, and always have been, gentle to the environment. The soapmaker of today can produce a product reminiscent of the old soap made in the kitchens, basements, and backyards by our ancestors. However today's soapmaker, in less than two hours can make a better looking, highly fragranced, naturally colored, and exfoliating soap. Making soap for profit can be a rewarding experience financially, esthetically, and ecologically.

Notes

Soap Making as a Business

How did you get started?

Hidden Meadows was the name of our llama farm. When my husband died suddenly, I had two infants and 40 llamas. I felt I needed to stay home and raise the children, so began looking at some alternatives in home businesses.

Outside the dining room window is a rather large herb garden. During the summer of 1995 it grew beyond my personal use. I had a pamphlet indicating various uses for herbs—soap and bath products were mentioned.

Never having been a very craft-oriented person, I invited my next door neighbor to join me in the venture—adventure—of making soap.

We ordered a soapmaking kit. When the kit arrived in September we very nervously began the process of making our first batch of soap.

Amazingly, it worked! We had made two kinds of soap—rose glycerin and vegetarian—following the directions to the letter. [2]

Did you do anything special before you started the soap business?

Before Hidden Meadows became an actual business we bartered and borrowed some of our supplies from family and friends. We had no idea how successful our venture would be.

Once established, we found wholesale houses for the essential oils and containers. We sought out wholesale groceries for some of our basic ingredients. We found old uncracked enamel pans in our grandmother's attics. From friends basements we confiscated old berry crates to display our soap. We recycled used bureau drawers to store the soap. Old Tupperware, juice cans, and PVC pipe were scavenged from resale stores, friends' kitchens, and garages.

When starting a business not all items necessary for production need be new.

[2] *The whole story is recorded in a small pamphlet "Diary of a Soapmaker" available through Kopacetic inK, PO Box 323, Kalama, WA 98625 for $5.00 including shipping and handling.*

Did you decide to have a business right away?

Hidden Meadows soap and bath products came about because of the quantity of soap we had produced in a few short weeks. We had more than 100 bars, squares and balls of soap. Family and friends seemed to really like the product and *asked* to buy it from us.

How did you begin marketing all that soap?

Even though Shelly had five children and I had two—we could only use so much soap and give away so many bars as gifts. We began looking for places to sell the soap.

Someone suggested we sell at local bazaars. We happened to make our first batches of soap at the right time for bazaars—the fall. By accident, we were ready for the holiday markets.

We signed up for several weekend bazaars in our home town and a community about fourteen miles away. Before the end of December we found ourselves in the black and in business. Three merchants had seen our products at the bazaar and wanted to sell them in their stores.

Did you do anything special to promote your business?

We were not thinking promotion in the beginning. Hidden Meadows was begun as a means to use our herbs and make a small profit. When we found ourselves, after just six weeks of making soap, in the black and in three stores—we began to look toward the future and a broader market place.

Did you have any kind of business plan?

Not in the beginning, we were just home crafters. When we found ourselves in eight stores and three states, we began to be more formal in looking at the future of Hidden Meadows. We developed a business plan.

What is a business plan?

Business plans are essential in having a successful business.

Business plans basically describe the business. They can be helpful in drafting proposals about the business if you need additional capital to start or continue the business.

A business plan examines where you are, where you are going, and how you will know when you get there.

A *formalized* business plan includes:

- Legal structure—sole proprietorship, corporation, or partnership
- Products of service—what is the consumer buying
- Potential market—who will buy the product
- Marketing plan—competition, pricing, industry trends, advertising
- Location of business
- Capital requirements—for beginning and continuation
- How you intend to raise the capital
- Financial projections
- Management
- Personnel requirements
- Insurance and security requirements
- Resumes of you and other key employees
- Obstacles to entering the marketplace
- How the obstacles can be overcome

That list appears intimidating!

Remember, the complete business plan is useful and necessary for any government, bank, or personal loan. The business plan becomes the vehicle to assist you in evaluating and re-evaluating the business.

What would you advise someone to do before they really started a business?

Talk to people who are in the business or a similar venture. Do not be afraid to check out the competition. Look through the Yellow Pages—is anyone offering the product? Are they local? Find stores which carry homemade craft items, gifts, or bath products. Explore your local market area first.

How did you check out the competition?

We attended the Seattle Market[3] about 140 miles away to see what other companies might be making and selling soap. We also went looking for a possible rep[4] and some alternatives to our packaging.

Was it worth the trip?

We found three companies who offered great suggestions in packaging some or all of our products. We noticed only three businesses selling homemade soaps and bath products. One particular group of reps were interested in our product if we could put more 'finesse' in our packaging.

It was worth the trip.

Did you have to do anything special to actually start Hidden Meadows?

I had a business license for Hidden Meadows llama farm already. I went to the Department of Labor and Industries and altered the name to Hidden Meadows Handcrafts and changed the focus of the business. The cost of a business license is minimal (@$25). The license let the State know we were in business. They send the necessary quarterly tax forms for us to fill out and send in.

---

[3] *Almost every major city holds a market twice a year for retailers to see and order merchandise. Check with retailers for dates and location of local marketplaces.*
[4] *A rep is a person who sells your product wholesale to merchants for a fee.*

Did you have to do anything else?

I checked with the Health Department for special needs or license—since soap was not consumed, we did not require a health permit.

I called my insurance agent for an umbrella policy to cover mishaps in making or using the soap.

Any special requirements for keeping track of expenses or income?

Knowing how to keep records is essential in managing a business. A computer, Quick Books, and Microsoft Excel software assist us in our bookkeeping as well as keeping track of the recipes!

How did you use them?

Quick Books creates invoices and purchase orders. The program also keeps track of payments received and a list of vendors as well as merchants.

In Excel spreadsheets include a:

· *General Ledger* which records *everything* on a daily basis
· Four *Quarter Sales* Sheets—helps me in processing sales tax and B & O taxes each quarter.
· *Expense Sheet*—keeps track of supplies
· *Cost Sheet*—actually breaks down the cost of products made
· *Consignment Sheet*—breaks down to whom and how much of what was given to sell
· *Out of Pocket Sheet*—since there were two of us in the beginning when one of us bought a little ribbon or a mold—instead of charging it to the business *per se* we kept track individually and used that information for our individual income tax returns.

What happened to your business plan?

Six months later it had to be revised. In the beginning we were making lip balm, bath crystals, massage and bath oils as well as soap. We were selling our products at fairs, bazaars, Saturday markets, and a few stores in the local area. Managing all those products was impractical. Shipping costs of the crystals and oils cut deeply into the retailer's profit margin, so we reduced our product line.

We now concentrate primarily on making soap. We still supply a few stores with other products, but only within a fifty mile radius.

Any other revisions to your business plan?

Currently we are exploring using the internet as a marketing/advertising tool. A friend posted our wholesale sheet on a llama bulletin board once. Because of her effort a new store is now handling our product!

Can you sum up how to start a business?

Find something you enjoy doing. Check out the competition. If you can figure out why someone would rather buy that service or product from you rather than the competitor start drafting a business plan.

Any last words of advise in starting a soap making business?

Don't start any business—including making soap—if you don't like doing it. We were hooked after the first attempt. Even after a few thousand bars of soap we still enjoy the creative side of soapmaking—experimenting with different herbs or essential oil combinations.

Our latest venture is making K-9 body bars—soap made with essential oils which repels and inhibits fleas. It is being sold through a pet store as well as at SitStay.com[5] on the web!

---

[5] *Http:///www.SitStay.com/store/health*

68

Resources

HERBS

Rodale's Illustrated Encyclopedia of HERBS, Rodale Press 1987

THE HERB BOOK, Arabella Boxer and Philip Back, Reed International Books Limited, 1980.

THE COMPLETE BOOK OF HERBS & SPICES, Lesley Bremness & Jill Norman, Viking Penguin, 1995.

G'S SEASONINGS COMPANY, 22344 NW 21 Place, Portland, Oregon 97210 *wholesale herbs/spices*

ESSENTIAL OILS

THE ART OF AROMATHERAPY, Pamela Allardice, NY: Crescent Books, 1995

COMPLETE AROMA THERAPY HANDBOOK: ESSENTIAL OILS FOR RADIAN HEALTH, Suzanne Fisscher-Rizzi, New York, NY: Sterling Publishing Co., 1990.

OTHER SOAP BOOKS

The Art of Making Soap, Merlyn Mohr, NY: Camden House Publishing, 1979.

The Natural Soap Book, Susan Miller Cavitch, VT: Storey Communications, 1995.

SOAP: MAKING IT, ENJOYING IT, Ann Bramson, NY: Workman Publishing , 1972, 1975.

THE SOAP BOOK, Sandy Maine, Interweave Press, 1995.

SOAP RECIPES, Elaine White, Starkville, MS: Valley Hills Press, 1995.

Index

Notes

Notes

Notes

Notes

Notes

Notes

Notes

Note About *the* Author

Hidden Meadows Handcrafts began in the fall of 1995 by accident. The author, Linda C. Inlow and her neighbor, Shelly Morgan made soap and other bath products in their kitchens. Family and friends enjoyed the results so much the two women formed Hidden Meadows and began to sell wholesale and low end retail.

Prior to this venture the author operated owned a llama ranch, dealt in real estate and taught at the local college. She continues to teach community education classes such as 'How to Start Your Own Business', 'First Time Home Buyers', and 'How to Get Published'. In 1996 she began offering the classes 'Soapmaking' and 'Use of Essential Oils' through the local Parks and Recreation Department, as well.

While managing the businesses Linda also raises her two children on a seven acre farm in a small rural community in Washington State. She spends her time writing, gardening, reading, teaching and of course making soap.

OTHER BOOKS BY THE AUTHOR INCLUDE:

Making the Most of Your Llama (Kopacetic inK)

Diary of a Soapmaker pamphlet(Kopacetic inK)

The Odd Lot: Raising Unusual Animals (Kopacetic inK)

Becoming Me: An Autobiography for the Reader to Complete (Kopacetic inK).

Becoming Me: A Journey Towards Self Discovery (Kopacetic inK).